BOA
EDITIONS LTD

YARD SHOW

YARD SHOW

Janice N. Harrington

AMERICAN POETS CONTINUUM SERIES NO. 210
BOA EDITIONS, LTD. * **ROCHESTER, NY** * **2024**

First Edition
23 24 25 26 7 6 5 4 3 2 1

For information about permission to reuse any material from this book, please contact The Permissions Company at www.permissionscompany.com or e-mail permdude@gmail.com.

Publications by BOA Editions, Ltd.—a not-for-profit corporation under section 501 (c) (3) of the United States Internal Revenue Code—are made possible with funds from a variety of sources, including public funds from the Literature Program of the National Endowment for the Arts; the New York State Council on the Arts, a state agency; and the County of Monroe, NY. Private funding sources include the Max and Marian Farash Charitable Foundation; the Mary S. Mulligan Charitable Trust; the Rochester Area Community Foundation; the Ames-Amzalak Memorial Trust in memory of Henry Ames, Semon Amzalak, and Dan Amzalak; the LGBT Fund of Greater Rochester; and contributions from many individuals nationwide. See Colophon on page 107 for special individual acknowledgments.

Cover Art: "Melrose Quilt" by Clementine Hunter
Cover Design: Sandy Knight
Interior Design and Composition: Isabella Madeira
BOA Logo: Mirko

BOA Editions books are available electronically through BookShare, an online distributor offering Large-Print, Braille, Multimedia Audio Book, and Dyslexic formats, as well as through e-readers that feature text to speech capabilities.

Cataloging-in-Publication Data is available from the Library of Congress.

State of the Arts

NYSCA

BOA Editions, Ltd.
250 North Goodman Street, Suite 306
Rochester, NY 14607
www.boaeditions.org
A. Poulin, Jr., Founder (1938-1996)

NATIONAL
ENDOWMENT
for the ARTS
arts.gov

It had been there for centuries, this yard-show tradition, but almost no one outside the culture knew about it, this not-for-our eyes cubism, fauvism, expressionism, surrealism, dada, abstract expressionism, pop, minimalism, graffiti, postmodern, neo-this, neo-that, neo-everything, or proto-everything.

—William Arnett

. . . some African Americans decorate, dress, or work their yards using a flexible visual vocabulary that creolizes and revitalizes American, European, and African traditions through everyday materials—tires, stones, twine, pinwheels, plumbing, planters, toys, and auto parts. . . . The makers of these special yards work to please themselves.

—Grey Gundaker

There aren't a lot of black people writing about the Midwest.

—Roxanne Gay

Contents

IV

V

VI

A WASP

settles on my eyelid—but
when is attention ever without risk?

YARD WORK

To shape a yard show,

to take her words—

only more of nothing
les' you do something with it—

as manifesto,
as compass, and please
no eye but my own.

A cement virgin painted black.

A plastic stallion's head hung on the shed wall.

Her words
used for yardstick, for measure—
for any bare, bereaved, or
unbearable—add *something*.

Tea roses ablaze on a white trellis.

Fires kindled amidst a time of fire,

and thorny canes meant
to *grab-a-holt* and hold on to,

hold fast despite so many losses,
so many lost, the roll of names.

This lesson: that attention
makes belonging, makes place.

Her mattock singing, and gut-driven
into ground trod hard-as-cement.

Yard work: to make,
to sow, sweep, hoe, meaning

to hone a word sharp enough
to stake claim or uproot.

The stallion whinnies,
or maybe it's only the wind.

I

To speak or write the world is to make it accessible to a reading, that is, to make it into a place.

—Stephen H. Daniel

BURN

The wind then, through seams of bluestem,
or switchgrass swayed by a coyote's passing.

Where the fabric gapes, Barthes said,
lies the sensual. A prairie cut

by winding seeps, or winds or shearing wings.
Mare's tails, mackerels, cirrus,

distance dispersed as light. Under a buzzard's bank
and spiral the prairie folds and unfolds.

Here between the stands of bluestem, I am interruption.
I rake my fingers over culms and panicles.

Here seeds burr into my sleeves, spur each hem.
In a prairie, I am chance. I am rupture. The wind—

thief, ruffian, quick-fingered sky—snatches a kink
of my hair. The broken nap falls, wound round

like a prairie snake, a coil of barbed wire, a snare
for the unwary. In the fall, volunteer naturalists

will wrench invading roots and scour grassy densities
with fire. Wick, knot, gnarl, my kindled hair

will flare, burn, soften into ash, ash that will settle,
sieve through soil, compost for roots to suck

and worms to cast out, out into the loess that raises
redtop, turkeyfoot, sideoats grama,

and all the darkened progenies of grass
that reach and strive and shape dissent from light.

PRAIRIE BLAZING STAR

after Carol Frost

Roman-candle, rod, exclamation point, quill—

Lillian's hand-written letters lie in an acid-free box.

How old her news has grown. The fields here resemble

the chalked lines drawn across childhood blackboards,

five lines, four rows. No one has good penmanship now.

The grass bends, trembles, sways. Such uncertainty.

What do bees hear exactly? I am a purse for ghosts,

a portmanteau, a satchel, a seed bag. Chords of heat

strike a fork of bluestem, strike the tines of culver's root.

A woman (Black, southern), her words (Black, southern)

preserved on archival paper. The original prairie

(rope-roots, net-roots), impermeable, could only be broken

by a steel blade. Words make the best sod. *Well*

the happiest moment of my life was when I was growing up

and the saddest when I got married. . . . A lot of things

I wanted and could not get them. Up close a blazing star

looks like a feather duster. Why would I save more words?

Beside the interstate, in a restored prairie, grow stands

of *coreopsis, St. John's wort, coneflower, blazing star.*

I read and re-read the words from a box of old letters.

I note each misspelling, the unknown names, the tone,

and the salutation. Is this restoration? If I set the pages

afire, as they burn the prairie to raise the dormant seed,

will new meanings rise? Her name was Lillian, two l's

like reaching arms, staves of tallgrass, torches maybe.

ANYTHING DARK BEARS THE NAME

Coneflower (*niggerhead, niggerheel*)

Queen-of-the-meadow (*nigger weed*), boneset (*nigger weed*)

Black-eyed Susans (*nigger tits, nigger thumbs, nigger daisy*)

Threadleaf sedge (*niggerwool*)

Greenbrier, dark trillium, Buckhorn plantain (*niggerheads*)

The red and yellow one? Indian blanket

(but also *nigger toes*)

KNOWING HOW TO LOOK

Wasn't nobody on that prairie
looked like me—

and yet—coneflower or Black Samson,
that new bluestem they call *prairie blues.*
Say, that new grass they call the prairie *blues.*

Micheaux's eye, and how his camera
read that black dirt: *He was young,*
      The Homesteader
—just passed twenty-two—and vigorous,
strong, healthy and courageous.

Brushy Fork, Brooklyn, Buxton,
Lyles Station, Pinhook, DeWitty,
always a church, always graves,
always some sign: Negro Creek, Negro Hill.

Wasn't nobody on that prairie
looked like me—

and yet Gordon Parks'
Black boy lying in a field of green
under scepters of thistle.

Wasn't nobody—and yet

bodies bound by razor wire,
Black bodies falling
above the ghost of a black-soil prairie.

as far as I could see, Hughes wrote,
. . . nobody . . .

—and yet—

by road, by rail, by resolution,
axles burdened with all they owned, they came,
moving like wind through tallgrass, wave after wave,
multitude and boundless and coming on.

WHEN IDENTIFYING TALLGRASS

      I set their stalks in a glass vase,
tallgrasses I do not know—spikes, panicles, racemes—

      the key is to look
at the structure of their seeds. As always the smallest part

      of the pattern shapes the form
that counts for everything. Tetsuya Fujita, in the aftermath

      of Hiroshima, studied blasted trees, seared
bones in a schoolyard: the forecast of future disasters.

      What figures, what patterns
make any life?

      What shaped my own?
Charles and Anna heading North in a yellow station wagon.

      Many thousands gone, going away from,
going toward. Think of the Great Migration as disruption,

or pattern recognition, *jump down turn around* and

      in the photo
her plaid skirt and bobby socks, his hands on the child's

      shoulder, the long windows of the back end,
the way they pose, everything repeating, saying aloud,

      this is an American Family,
which is what they wanted, and why they left. Given

      the blast zone, the debris of '63, why stay?
A third wave, their own middle passage North:

how far they traveled in a day, where they stopped
or couldn't stop, tires beating what might be, might be.

The grasses? Prairie switchgrass,
Canadian rye, and sideoats grama, but I could be wrong.

THE WORD YOU'RE LOOKING FOR

What's the word
for the kind of loneliness that can feel like swimming
unassisted in a foreign language, for the very first time?
—Carl Phillips

You have made me think that there are other kinds.
Say, strolling by oneself through a tallgrass prairie
when everything is distant or beyond the eye,
that moment when a redwing trills a tag of notes
and then unanswered goes on. Or maybe the worry
of colored pencils over the paper's tooth, an empty page
and thus hungry, like the sound of my father's pencils
when he drew. I heard that hushed scraping once, sharp
pencil points scurrying back and forth, the friction of his breath
against a cardboard canvas similar to a poet's breath
over a keyboard. Could that sound serve
for loneliness? Low, soft, pushed out—breath planed, filed—
against an emptiness, but maybe on that imagined page
there are a few words, words that have no breath as yet, but
that once spoken, will take any breath, a sigh, a whisper,
an erupting shout. And reading the words aloud, isn't that—
the act of tucking your words into another's breath—
a kind of loneliness, a kind of theft?
If words must be breathed again, again—say these!
But some loneliness in that—right? Some searching?
Lonely—what comes like breathing, or the scrape of a pencil, or
maybe the damn pheasant that burst now from a stand of bluestem
to break the morning, to startle my heart into a faster beat, to make
my heart loud in my ears, then quiet, quiet enough to hear
that it's just me here and these extravagant grasses—I see
through slanting and arcs and buttresses, but not beyond
or over them: green, and bright-lifted, reaching, but not toward me.

WIND SHEAR

Under the magnolia, a winter-starved hare stills
and pretends it is not there,

and wanting less of fearfulness
I pretend that I do not see my camouflage, the wild promises
in my gaze, and step carefully by.

Morning, bitter morning—
lack and awful patience wait at every compass point.
Mourning, mournful, the prairie seals wind-scored stems with snow.

Here inside a stalk of goldenrod
a gall wasp will ride hard winter out.

Here between my ribs, wasps of lonely, wasps of
not yet, not yet wait and ride hard winter out.

Such a slow season, laggard and mean.
I can't explain the cardinals I've seen of late,

but the crows' black fists, the way they bully
eave and air, stab the morning with the sharpest *awe,*

I understand it now. I see the reason and agree.

II

This ability to hold on, even in very simple ways, is work Black women have done for a very long time.

—Alice Walker

The most monumental aspect of material culture—the use of space.

—Theresa A. Singleton

YARD SHOW I

African American yard shows are powerfully
rhetorical spaces where dross is turned into gold,
where ordinary materials are sanctified, and where
space is consecrated.

—John Beardsley

1

I should have paid attention—

to flowered urns lined in solemn symmetry
along the drive, to Peter Pan in painted knickerbockers,
to his cement fingers cupped to painted lips
calling what query, what answer?
Whose distant ear?

I should not have dismissed
as déclassé or disavowed

plaster ducks and plastic hens,
a pug, a lion cub, two ponds, three fountains,
all the wrought-iron filigree and sconces,
but should have weighed instead her argument, denial
of restraint or boundary beyond her own.

Black Versailles, Black baroque: ado, outdo,
and overdone. No minimal or less.

I don't like a whole lot of space.
It looks bare till you put something in it.

2

(**Beauty**, see also)

1. Intersectionality of property rights and identity formation in Black women.
2. The Great Migration and the influence of Southern folkways on African American gardening.
3. The impact of the Black Feminine on the American landscape.
4. Urban renewal and the erasure of local Black hegemony.
5. Black gardening as ideological resistance to neo-colonization and white supremacy.
6. See also yard art, vernacular landscape design, dressed yards, yard shows, spirit gardens, material song.

See—beauty, or what I know
I've got a right to.

3

Didn't her yard trouble?

Didn't her hanging baskets
and red bricks
say *Look!* Say, *I'm here.*

Didn't the hoe she drove
into that black dirt, drove
that time into a snake's spine,

prove that this space—*this
right here*—belonged to her?

4

When it gets bad, I just get out there in my garden.
Get to digging and the world just goes away.

World, she said, meaning *All that mess*
outside her gate that she tried to sway
with concrete swans, birdbaths,
and a red-capped gnome—

yard work, spirit work, woman's work.

5

Figure 43
Accession # 521
Shape: Aphrodite of Milos
Type: Cement lawn ornament
Decorative technique: white paint
Date range of manufacture: c.1970-1980s
Archaeological provenance: front yard

Discussion: A cement white woman in a front yard, atop a brick plinth, in Nebraska, beside a red oak that the owner planted, beside a red brick bungalow c. 1910. Classical female body: modest breast, sensual slope of waist and hip, armless.

Whiteness—she claims, uses. A frame, a spotlight, a tool for guiding the eye where she chose. *I was always too white for one side and not white enough for the other. There wasn't anyone who liked me.* Aphrodite beside her red, red roses. *Something to bring out the yard,* point to all she has done, made and remade as her own. *I've never needed a lot of people.* Third-Wave Migration: assemblage: traditional yard show and folkways: racial artifacts: the remnants of.

6

Come with me, she says. *Help me feed the fish.*
We go to her backyard pond,

the one she dug before he could come home
to *Tell her what to do,*

the one she saw in her mind.
I knew what I wanted. Didn't need a blueprint.

We sit and gaze into goneby, watch
another Aphrodite rise, from the long ago, in bobby socks

and penny loafers, belly swollen with her first child.
Who can tell me what beauty is, Fanon asked.

She asks, *Aren't they pretty?*
The fish come for pellets spilled from a plastic scoop.

They come for her laughter, though the water
distorts the notes. Pleasure a language

the light speaks, a language this Black woman
knows and has tried for so long, so long to teach.

7

The interstate sliced through predominately
African-American neighborhoods. . . . [M]ost of the
garden's features have been erased.
                                        —Paul Mullins

But isn't any Black woman's garden ephemeral?

~

Beware of Dog.

   Property protected by . . .

      Chain link fences around the perimeter.

      Steel padlocks.

~

In her yard:

      plastic waterfalls spill into plastic pools, tea roses,

      bronze dolphins leaping beside a brick well,

      bird houses, a concrete Dionysus whitened with paint.

      Tin basins tipped and staggered into fountains.

They think Black people don't have anything.
They think it's all slums.

~

Volition, maybe, or freedom—yes, free

at last, free at last, free now to do and undo. She denies—boundary,

and the fear made by boundaries, and refutes her fear

of snakes. She kills them here, in the Promised Land she's made

and filled with plastic leaves: to refuse rot, and season,

and grieving after. *Needs some green to give it life.*

Green and green and green—like a fist to beat the eye,

her roses loud as Sunday shouts, believers

bearing witness. O yes, Lord!

~

Ceramic chickens under the boughs of a crabapple.

A parcel of plastic deer beside a potted forest.

The plastic cardinal perched on the head of a nymph.

A metal stork with no neck or head beside an empty fountain.

A concrete German shepherd guarding a wrought-iron gate.

A plaque carved with "Flowers are love's truest language"

set in a flowerless urn.

~

And in the side yard—a bowling ball

on a plastic pedestal: pretense

of gaze, and view, and reflection—

the eye and its measure reject

any feigned foreseeing.

Witch ball. Gazing ball. Spirit ball.

Shaped urethane on a plastic pier for

seeing past, present, future—or wanting

to—all laughable, perhaps.

8

Milk cans and a cast iron kettle pinked with sedum, the garbage lid set beneath a statue of a mother and child. *Perhaps everybody has a garden of Eden, I don't know;* James Baldwin wrote, *but they have scarcely seen their garden before they see the flaming sword,* which might explain her habit to save and savor, her savage holding and holding on: the cement cacti on plastic posts, the poor putto with its broken skull. Everywhere broken things redeemed, reused, repurposed, nothing abandoned. The way she chops every garter snake into reticulated chunks. The way she painted her Jophiel—a plastic cherub—black. The flaming sword? Her roses maybe: long, sharp-thorned, burning near every gate.

9

Herculean: to hold, to make, to claim

a rose. Though her garden was never

just its beauty, but always foil

and remedy for loss, for less

than, for that assumed poverty.

They think Black people don't have anything.

10

A Black woman's yard as cure and testament

and *tour de force*, as hallowed ground

—though we never recognized the canvas

she labored over. *I'm particular,* she said,

to ears that never heard her meaning:

particular, choosy, but always her choice.

We never called her artist. We ignored,

scorned, scathed what she built there,

her wild, original, unfettered making.

No one studied her lived aesthetic,

or read in topiaries and painted sculpture

a manifesto: *I like to do it my own way.*

No one thought Giverny, Casa Azul, or

Aix-en-Provence, or said opus—

it was just a yard, flowers,

and lawn ornaments.

This Black *particular.*

This Black woman—

pleasing no one but herself.

The manifestation of the wind of thought is not knowledge; it is the ability to tell right from wrong, beautiful from ugly.

—Hannah Arendt

Icons in the yard show may variously command the spirit to move, come in, be kept at bay, be entertained with a richness of images or be baffled with their density.

—Robert Farris Thompson

PAUSING BESIDE HER YARD

I slow, I still—
                    before raptorial legs,

a mantis, luminous and green, on a concrete rim,

such dangers in the feints and meetings of bright shells,

such peril in a pause—

[*dawdle.   delay.   delight.*

The musician's rest. The erotic

that rises from Barthes' interruption

and Yi-Fu Tuan's proposition: place is a pause
                                              in movement.]

I move, I shift,

my fingers lift, lower,   pause
on a slope of hip and, restless,
                    settle: belong.

[*A pause, a hesitation,*

our doubt and uncertainty.]

We don't know, we know we don't,
and yet—
                    a pause

before moving forward,   anyway.

THE ART OF PORCH SWINGING

Six shot on a porch in Cleveland.

A three-year-old shot on her parents' front porch.

Fearing unrest, police clear the street,
fire paint rounds at porch watchers.

———

If memory is the stoop and its steps
—will you go in or out?

What if we call memory
the art of porch swinging?

"Scrubbed porches that sag and look their danger,"
Hansberry wrote, adding later:
"each piece of our living is a protest."

———

Neither part of nor away from: a porch.
Neither in nor out: a porch.
Where seeing is warrant, is say-so: a porch.

———

Come and we'll sit in that old way
"talking softly on this porch," as the poet said,

"with the snake plant in the jardiniere."
Sit beside me. We'll use our eyes
for boundary stones. *Whose child is that?*

Y'all know better. Making all that mess.

Not in the streets, but studying them, retelling
the stories that streets tell, nodding our heads,

our work, our bond. *Em-hm—*
we see you. Y'all know we see you.

TO THE WHITE GIRL WHO SCOLDED ME
THAT NOT EVERYTHING IS ABOUT RACE

The moon is in its highest seat.
   We try to position the telescope.
You insist it's the Sea of Tranquility. Dust on the lens, I say.

Over the tree marigold,
a hummingbird hovers, then winks away.

I think the large blue-white trumpets
are morning glories?

Such silly cabbage moths. Sufi-dancing, they whirl,
and, whirling, they listen and listen and listen.

Samiyah has a collection of mussel shells
on her front porch: *heelsplitters*, *fatmuckets*,
and *three-horned wartybacks*.

My brother left us years ago,
refuses now to speak to anyone.

Particulate, *splendiferous*, *skillet*, *jubilee*.

I truly believe the tallgrasses are beautiful,
the way they daven and lift their seedy panicles.

A ruined art installation releases its plastic cups, mylar,
and cellophane over the reconstructed prairie.

I am not adopted and yet I am
not the same skin color as my mother or my father.
How do they know me? How do they call me daughter?

Rise and bow down. Rise and bow down.
O Pilgrims—don't you feel
                              the light on your face?

Whatever happened to that garter snake? The one
that left such a lengthy sentence beside the garden hose?

No, I said. *Not everything.*

A SHINING LURE

Beside the back porch
a crow hangs a string of meat
from the magnolia's limb.

Poor garter snake, poor
ribbon, no longer container

for the reptilian. But still
your scales shine, still

they school—that we might
(couldn't we? shouldn't we?)
by shining lure

or by the clemency
of our body's brief flare
deny, fend off, or pierce
that coming dark.

IS IT BEAUTY THAT WE OWE?

I stir a glass bottle filled with glass beads
and remember your lesson: to leave a flaw,
one bead to break the pattern, to free the maker.
Not an error but humility: We are not gods.
The last bead molded into a fist, a grit,
a clog that stops the machine: No tidy endings!
Wrong color, wrong shape, wrong size,
the last bead set like a door or a period
or the stone before the tomb's mouth. Pattern
revealed as fraud and feint. I purposely
err, as you taught me, and choose odd, and
ugly, and unlike, and into every making
I weave fault, disruption, ember.

ON SEEING A PHASMA GIGAS

1

In adamant clarity, in an acrylic cube,
the one called phasma or ghost, difficult to see
on its native bark, compels and says I am,
repels and says I am. Which camouflage is which?

Stunned by extravagant repugnance, by alien
symmetry, I study its mottled wings,
the long, segmented abdomen— a thickened twig
to burn for fire, a rod for bruise or rule.

2

Letter to Philip Rau
from the Black entomologist, Oct. 29, 1914.

Dear Mr. Rau:

I desire [   ]

[   ] but   cannot [   ]

[   ] long to say [   ] but
I know so little
                          about [   ] less
about [   ] and   nothing
[   ] beyond the grave [   ]
[   ] ponder [   ] I must

confess, however, [   ] not [   ] understand.
What is [   ]? What is beyond [   ]
Eternal [   ] or eternal [   ]   which?

How I long [   ]. At times

I am almost persuaded.

Yours sincerely,
C. H. Turner

3

Even in a phasma gigas: redemption,
that it has made the eye falter, stop, turn,
that it has stilled the mind's restlessness
and covered its questions with sticky eggs.

The phasma gigas disappears: twig, bark, a stain
of light, or lack,

and isn't it lack, or want, or absence
that seduces, lures, releases at last?

4

He feared spiders, my father, ran screaming
at the touch of one. Cried like a baby, she said.

Is that what she said? *Just as scared*
as he could be. Neva did like them.

White cottony eggs in my basement corner,
so many, so many. *Don't kill them,*
my mother said. *It will bring bad luck.*

The translucent spiders that live in the corners
of my ceiling have adapted themselves to painted stucco,
to dust, and incandescent light.

That shadow? It could be a spider.
It could be a brown recluse.
It could be my nappy hair.

5

Charles H. Turner wrote
that spiders were not machines—not,
as Stein might have said a web, a web, a web, a web.

A funnel-weaver spider
lowered into the aorta of a human heart
will weave a web appropriate for the space.

We love each other and so the web
has a human shape.

What if my touch is not affection but only hunger?
Rub your skin-web against my skin-web: listen.

6

My favorite story explains the origin
of the spider's web. The animals owed
a debt, but it fell to spider to pay it,
and so spider wove lace to sell at the market,
hung its fine linens over limbs and leaves.

Walking beside the prairie, I ask if you see
the thin strings cat-cradled between
slants of bluestem, gold spans,
ties, snares, garlands of sunlight.
Look, I say. Look. Do you see them?

Webs.
A strand of spittle winds from an ailing lip.

Web-based content management systems.

Against my breast, a strand of your grey hair,
the light striking it.

Look!
a spider is paying my debt.

7

In Papua, New Guinea a child brings a phasma gigas
to show the stranger.

Find more, the stranger says, more spiders, butterflies,
beetles. Find more. And he promises—always—to pay.

YARD SHOW II

A woman's backyard and garden.

What she's made, with coins of sweat and constant work:
      genius loci, hierophany, sanctum.

Blue dayflowers in a rusty kettle.

No, I have never spoken there with the unseen.

     ≈

She told me that she almost died once.
It was just like falling asleep, just as peaceful.

The plastic rock beside the back gate said *Learn to forgive.*
The field stones, red quartzite, said nothing.

     ≈

A monarch perched on the lip of a rose.

     ≈

Maybe the voice of the unseen sounds like a hoe blade
chopping hard ground or a woman ripping out deep roots.

A yard? Because a body needs to stop sometime.   (rest)
Do you ever feel weary and long for rest?   (rest)
A mind surrounded by beauty is a mind at rest.   (rest)
A mind at rest goes back. She said, *My mind goes back.*   (rest)

     ≈

A green bangle looped round an ankle of light.
Answer: garter snake.

≈

Yard, yard art, yard decoration, yard show,
vernacular environment, vernacular landscape,
home ground, spirit garden, material prayer . . .

Psyche, soul, pneuma—I like container best.
But what contains also restrains.
Free yourself, or you'll never be free.

And so those hussies, the petaled harlots
she planted everywhere, loud and brazen,
with no stoppin' sense: that freedom
to be—a prideful thing, all swagger and satisfied.

≈

Without trouble, and death, no beauty . . .
—John Ruskin

Was Ruskin talking about a woman's yard?
About a Black woman's yard?

A woman in her garden with a hoe.
Chop, chop-a-row, chop.

Or maybe it was *No death without beauty and trouble?*

A woman in her garden with a hoe.
Mr. Death come along, and she refused to go.

Memento vitae: rust-red sedum in a white-washed tire.
Memento mori: a wasp, a wasp's venom.

IV

People don't make the journeys to come and die, they make them to come and live. And to live you transform the place.

—John Akomfrah

THERE IS A PRICE

Acka backa soda cracka acka backa boo

or *boom* or *ka-boom!*
Four girls blown apart in *Bombingham,*

Yellow and chrome, long-bodied, a station wagon heads North.

History is potholed with tedium:
going by, going by, going.

In the trunk, the past lies bundled tight in a strip quilt. The present's slipping
gear, and the future splayed on the shoulder: bodies ruptured, broken by bodies
in motion.

Deer, dogs, birds—carcasses left for light or beak or maggot. Endless collisions
and ricochets—the small white crosses and plastic flowers say: something
happened. It happened here. Something always gets broken. It's the price paid,
the tax. They go on.

Everyone does.

Family as kudzu   family as weather and roof
that ol' Mason-Dixie   where they stopped, where they held their breath
night, dog-baying night   *came up on the edge of a tornado*

Came up in '64
But then all roads are toll roads.

They paid.   Though their children paid more.
                 No one ever said it, but

they knew.

WHAT PLACE IS THIS? WHERE ARE WE NOW?

Here the prairies—Round, Carthage, Bushnell,
Hancock—that sheltered the runagate,
black shadows slipping through, stealing away,

hiding in the thick brush behind stands of tallgrass.
Hush now, hush. Quiet as moonlight tip-toein'
over the tines of turkeyfoot. Hush.

By *prearranged signals . . . the distinct drumming
. . . of a prairie chicken, or the bark of a prairie wolf*
—runaways step from stands of bluestem,
                                                    hurry, hurry-
ing on to the next station, going north,
all the way to the Promised Land.

                              *

Dredges. Drainage tiles. Plows. Barbed wire.
By 1900, the Illinois prairies were gone.

Read Sandburg's question—*What place is this?*
another way—without bluestem, Indiangrass,
or switchgrass, without that green
and swelling sea—*Where are we now?*

                              *

A journalist wrote that prairie roots broken
by the self-scouring steel plow
sounded like *a fusillade of pistols.*

                              *

On a city map, blooms of color mark
each gun death.

The new billboard begs
     Put the Gun Down,
and shows the image of a Black man.

Pile them high at Gettysburg, Sandburg said.
Pile them high at Ypres and Verdun.

I am the grass
let me work.

*

At the Illinois River Correctional Center,
Black prisoners plant seedlings:
Black Samson, black-eyed Susan, black snakeroot.
They pot ironweed and iron butterfly.

Behind cinderblock walls and razor wire, Black men
learn of grasses higher than a man's head, imagine
boundless green and nothing over them but sky.

MEMOIR OF A HERITAGE TOURIST

1

On I-72 heading west—

could take exit 133A to forgotten coal wars:
the Pana massacre, the Battle of Virden,
Black and immigrant laborers,
ruthless capital, and troops
summoned to stay the bleeding,

or in any direction old Black codes,
sundown towns, and closed covenants,

exits 138 or 144 to the nearest
correctional facilities (five more
in driving distance)

—but I am heading to Springfield,
through flatscapes, past variegated greens,
the Second Amendment Burma-shaved on fence posts

    SHOOTING SPORTS

    ARE SAFE AND FUN

    THERE'S NO NEED

    TO FEAR A GUN

while a voice on the radio predicts farm futures.

2

In a filling station remade as a museum
for Roots Tourism, I study *The Negro Motorist Greenbook.*

Black folks leaving. That audacity—to leave,
faith enough to snatch their bodies elsewhere.
First Wave, Second Wave migrations
following the road and its minstrel shows,
knowing where darker bodies *could* or *could not*.

Get Your Kicks on Route 66,
Nat King Cole—his hair conked and tar-
shiny—smiles the lyrics. Every Black ear
listens to the unspoken irony and the warning.

3

Blackened windows. A blackened door.
At the edge of Springfield's old Black district:

The Lincoln Colored Old Folks and Orphans Home,
a red brick Italianate where sixty to seventy
children, elders, and disabled squeezed
into six bedrooms and a basement,

where Miss Eva Monroe held on
from Teddy's Rough Riders to Ethel Waters
on the radio lamenting *Stormy Weather.*

Say a Tuskegee airman tried to save it,
make it into a tourist attraction. He died.

Good work, good trouble—
to save and to keep, at least to try?

Frederick Douglass in 1888: *Colored people . . .*
are bound to keep the past in lively memory
till justice shall be done them. Bound, he said.

4

Bound and boxed in an upstairs closet—
what we carried North: letters, a ragdoll, a quilt, a pocket watch,
fading photographs, and in this Depression-era schoolbook
a Black girl's stories and notes.

> *Lamar County Training School:*
>
> Henry Walker, Lillian Hollis, Annie Allmon,
> Else Boman, Jaine Hoffer, Addie Johnson, Ruby Walker, Charlie Boman;
>
> hand-colored maps of the western states;
>
> her words *Silver moonlight made a path across the lake.*

In a cardboard box lie keepsakes, keepsafes,
the pages time-scorched—even tenderness abrades.

Tomorrow, I'll buy acid-free tissues
and museum-quality boxes. I'll secure the words
of a Black girl passed down,
that justice owed her, that bond.

PEMBROKE TOWNSHIP, ILLINOIS I

1. *We visit a community of Black farmers south of Chicago to conduct interviews. We talk of race and, losing our way, we approach by another route.*

2. *An endless invisible present going on,* Giscombe writes.

3. *Flat. Clouds set like table runners. Rain predicted. Spring fields in every direction: rows and rows of black.*

4. In our second interview, a local woman speaks of outsiders and ATVs rutting ancient sands. She speaks of weekenders with glocks, semi-automatics, shotguns, city strays flung from car windows, and poachers (rare plants, seeds, birds). They even steal our *snakes.*

5. *Black boughs, rain-black leaves. The trail abandoned, overgrown.*

6. I meet a Black Midwestern farmer: tall, stately, she modeled once. *Ma'am,* she said, because I was the elder: this respect, this endless invisible Blackness: meaning, I see you. Her courtesy: I see you.

WITH THE WALLS REMAINING

Springfield, Illinois

The letters **H O T E L** cling in lead paint
despite scouring winds and scathing sun,
another "ghost sign" for my archive.

But I've come to see Preston Jackson's monoliths,
his bas-reliefs mirroring the iconic photograph:
Springfield Race War, Aug. 1908,
the shell of fire-gutted walls standing at riot's end,
one of many *Acts of Intolerance:*
brown bodies cowering in cornfields, hiding
by the hundreds in the state arsenal.

The Black district engulfed in 5,000 angers.
Mobs charging down Madison, Jefferson,
and Washington Streets, white men howling
"Throw him to the fire! Throw him to the fire!"

Now, many summers later, the same streets
furnace other fires: The Housing Authority,
the Urban League, the Salvation Army
Adult Rehabilitation Center. *Free HIV Testing,*
Know Your Status, and *Cash paid*
for diabetic strips. The homeless gather
in the meager shade of brick walls, giving
no heed to another tourist or her camera.

> **Home of Lincoln 1840**
> **City of Lincoln, Capital of Illinois**

The historical marker does not say: You could hear
the body's heels knocking against the trunk,

does not say that men took pieces
of the tree for souvenirs.

At the base of the marker, my camera
captures a patch of white clover,
a wreath, a garland. So many
wreaths from troubled soil,
so many names on that bloody roll,
so many children lifting cardboard placards:

Black Lives Matter

And children too in Jackson's monument,
holding hands and marching.
Black bodies bronzed and alloyed with silence,
following the drummer's tattle:
a-gi-tate, a-gi-tate, a-gi-tate.

On Jackson's *Acts of Intolerance,* the walls
rise from an inferno, do what walls always do:
witness, shelter, defy.

But on another wall, near the depot
where Lincoln departed for Washington,
I study a second ghost sign. The letters offer

FIRE PROOF STORAGE

History's work, a warning of coming fires,
a wall trying again, as walls do,
to save something from the flames.

PEMBROKE TOWNSHIP, ILLINOIS II

7. Emerald green, gold-feathered shoulders shot with ribbons of onyx: when
    was rooster ever the right word? Better cock or cockerel, better silkie. This
    is what light would look like, *if it could strut.*

8. Goldfish in black water. PVC pipes reshaped into a hydroponic
    agricultural hydration and growth system: raising produce for the Chicago
    suburbs.

9. In memory's pond a glint of koi and one black catfish. [Story: Sun and
    Moon asked to send away their children—too bright, too hot, too many.
    Sun turned her children into fish and sent them to swim in the waters of
    the earth. But Moon could not, would not. Why not hide them? *Listen,
    Child, listen. Come out only at night.* Babies as pale-skinned as their moon
    mother. So many, so many. The sun is still angry.]

10. Giscombe writes

    > *memory divides, then itself dogs*
    > *all the shapes at once, the dense edges of them,*
    >   *the empty hearts . . .*

11. Dog-maimed, this ewe hobbles on three legs, the wrenched and injured
    leg, held up, will not bear her weight. The kid suckles, pulls and pulls at
    the rubbery nipple.

12. A cicada shell clings to the trunk of a black oak. Filled with light (a
    lantern), filled with rain (a chalice), filled with dust (*you know the answer,
    admit you know it*).

PEMBROKE TOWNSHIP, ILLINOIS III

13. If I choose not to say impoverished? If I don't say third-world or poorest in the nation? Is the lack of running water or a flush toilet poverty or wealth? Theory projects its shadows, directs the light.

14. They said—quiet, that they loved the quiet. But who would allow a Black woman to crave silence? To find succor or solace in quietude? Hush, let the noise pass over you.

15. A lark sparrow whistles *pip-pip-pip*.

16. In the children's section, the librarian showed us her collage, images reassembled from old magazines: a pomegranate blossom and blackberry petals pinned to a Black girl's hair.

17. Black oaks. Black limbs grasping all that blue, refusing to let go, to lose anything more.

18. *Each landscape has a black edge to it*—Giscombe argues.

19. What makes blackness here? The road, the bark of a black oak, the charred carcass of a single-wide, a Black woman's eye?

AMERICAN STANDARD

Pembroke Rodeo, Illinois

This cowgirl and horse a-gallop, a-
gallop around the corral, the *living* standard
unfurled and held straight by a Black hand
and born solemnly around the ring.
But these elders, Black and grayed, give
the pageantry no special regard, neither
standing, nor covering their hearts,
nor singing, nor waving, nor raising a cheer
or even pointing a lens. The bright
cloth passes by while others clap or stand.

But oh how they cheer for the Union's blue
and the Buffalo Soldier, how they cheer
the Black men herding stallions and steers
and cheer for each barrel rider, and louder still
and longer for the men—unable to throw their steer—
who hold on, twisting the muscled neck again,
wrenching it back, tightening their grip, leaning
in until the heavier body falls. The old folks
cheer then, Black women clapping loud
to mark the victory, the holding on and trying
again. They set no clock on the doing.

THROUGH A MOBILE LENS, BROOKLYN, ILLINOIS

In the distance, St. Louis and its Arch:
gateway to the west, national
expansion, and what not, said the architect.

A Crime Stoppers billboard as you enter.
Barges bearing corn hybrids, coal,
recycled plastics.

Trust God   Gun Show July 9 & 10

Scabs of linoleum atop a cement slab.
Everywhere: *once* or *used-to-be*,
the mobile present and its double-wide.

Soft drink and chips
passed through a slot
in the bulletproof glass.

Home is not a place,
Baldwin wrote, *but . . . an irrevocable condition.*

The face peering
out of the driver's window
of a speeding patrol car.

Projects? Turn west after Lovejoy Elementary School.
Elijah Lovejoy: *I shall hold myself at liberty to speak.*

Quinn Chapel AME	*Fantasyland*
Lovejoy Temple	*ROXXX*
Transforming Word Church	*Bottom's Up*
First Free Will Baptist Church	*Dawg Pound Gentlemen's Club*
St. Elizabeth Temple	*Peek a Boo*
First Corinthian Missionary Baptist	*Pleasure Palace*

Before the war, Robert E. Lee
fixed Bloody Island to Illinois.

A matter of where you redirect
the currents: what gets by-
passed or who.

Oldest Black Town in America

Sunlight fills the empty lots.
Behind every half-drawn curtain, watchful eyes.

FLOOD PLAINS

1

Sangamon, Vermilion, Middlefork, Kaskaskia,
Embarras, Douglas, Salt Fork, Jordan.

The complex drama of competing surface tensions, Sedgwick writes, *keeps the water surface breathing, shifting, expanding, and self-enfolding.*

Black bodies
behind razor wire
(40 minutes—
maybe 20)

Beside the Sangamon,
flood waters surge
past soybeans, silos, corn-processing plants,
abandoned coal mines, pump-jacks,
and all the ruined prairies.

2

If you want to influence the design on this evolving surface at all, Sedgwick writes further, *you can do so with a soft breath . . .*

The nearest
sundown town
(9 miles)

Soft the trail, soft the earth,
we hike through Fox Ridge
over a glacier's calligraphy,
ridgebacks, ravines, and the muddy
meander of the Embarras.

3

What results is a snapshot of a living spatial dynamic—

A now forgotten
lynching
(32 miles)

Turkey buzzards circling,
a-glide on a heated draft.
Midwestern memento mori.

He forgot the key
to his aunt's house.

A wake, a kettle, a committee—
buzzards with their nostril-windows.

Burglary in process.
Shots fired.
(2 miles)

In every direction death-stink.

4

One that, like the . . . self-similar bifurcations of roots, branches, and capillaries in a tree,

The tracks
that bore Till
to Money,
Mississippi
(2 blocks)

Bifurcations. Division. Separate.
I stopped for gas.
Small-town eyes, a pickup that refused
to slow or wait for me to pass, forcing me to hurry.
Dark waters swell, rise into flood-rage.

5

or of rivulets in a delta, is a veritable badge of chaos

The latest billboard
Put the Guns Down
(1 mile)

or perhaps an answer to chaos:
At Kaufman Lake, old Black men
cast lines and read shadows,
a difficult art to stand prayer-quiet, to wait.

Coal ash, benzene, lead
and arsenic.
(In the Northside,
near the tracks.)

Intent beside local waters,
taking stories or the thoughts that come
from slow waters, a bounty caught
or sometimes breaking the line.

20. Mulberries, wild plums, blackberries—sweetness carried in sparrow's gut and shat here. How do you know it wasn't the sparrow's song, and not the sparrow's shitting, that sowed the berry?

21. How to measure poverty? Can I know by looking at, or looking from, or looking over?

22. Everywhere, the sand thatched with wild strawberries. Where to step? And the story she told. Her son's insistence: They didn't need a radio, already had music. Cicadas. Bees. A Towhee's *Drink your tea! Drink your tea!*

23. In Pembroke, a woman walks beside a gravel road, plucking blackberries from roadside canes. Black fingers stained with purple ink, writing what and where they will.

ON THE ROAD TO THE OLD NEGRO CEMETERY

Relentless sky. The distance gauzed in hazy white
over bare fields.

I go in search of a story of other bodies
that scarred the prairie, prairies blackened
by fire, stirring buried seed.

Corn. Freight. Anhydrous Ammonia. Coal trains
a hundred cars long, set in a running stitch beside a hedgerow of osage.

Hawks perched on weathered posts, a constant scrutiny,
so many staring eyes.

       Pesotum

              I-57 South to Memphis, then I-36.

            Tuscola

Sundown curfews. A remembered sign in an alley off Main Street—
Don't let the sun set on you here. I don't stop.

Syngenta Seeds. Part-time work, maybe.

       Camargo

          Murdock

            Newman

No trespassing in every direction.

After a tight bend, rounding stubblefields speared with broken cornstalks,
bare, black soil hemmed by ditch banks and hidden tiles,
beside a scrap of withered prairie—I find it: The Old Negro Cemetery.

NANCY
wife of
L. JAMES
DIED
SEPT. 19, 1860
AGED 78 YEARS

Pennies, quarters, nickels left by visitors, a hundred or so.
How to explain that need
to leave these tokens? Why did I?

Difficult soils platted and given deed.
Through a stand of black cherry, shingle oaks, and black hickories,
I walk the crooked gut of Brushy Fork Creek, the dry, empty
border of other unseen graves, their shallow sinking in the earth.

The wind fretful in the switchgrass, that slight trembling.

*

The petition to rename it "Freedom Lane Cemetery" never took hold.
Whose discomfort?
Who decided?

White stone broken in a black field.
Eventually, white grit.

I leave my pilgrim's badge and turn back—
open space, unending acres,
none of it saying *stay*.

V

The passage of time is necessary for the experience of place.

—Robin Doughty

NIGHT FISHING

1

To dream of catching fish, says
Madame Sophronia's Unabridged Dictionary
of Ten Thousand Dreams, is to dream
that the powerful will favor you.

2

Beside Hickman Lake this portrait: a family fishing. A husband and wife bait
steel hooks, fishing while their children wait and do what children do when
every hour is stagnant water.

If I say it was a *Negro* family, what changes? If I say it was the year they found
a fourteen-year-old boy tethered like a fish in the waters of the Tallahatchie, or
the year Hayden wrote "In the cold spring night / the smelt are spawning," or if
I say the parents were weary and weary and weary and had mouths to feed, what
changes?

Bullhead, flathead, channel catfish. Three brown children sprawl on a cotton
sheet: one child lies in slack-mouthed sleep, one child pokes a spider with a
crooked stick, and one child watches the threading of a night crawler's hearts
(each one, each one, each one, each one, each one), studies the dark-skinned
water looking back at her, listens to its low mutter against the shore.

When you tell it, say the children walked into the algae-slimed waters of a lake.
Say their parents did not stop them. Say the water closed over their heads and
they grew fins and barbs. This is a story, so it is true.

They are fish now. Three catfish that love the rain's improvisations and anything
by Muddy Waters. Over a strand of monofilament, they listen to the faint
electric music of their parents' patience. They refuse to take up their human
bodies, to stand as their parents stood with hooks baited—corn, dough,

minnows, and five-hearted minutes—and eyes pinned to a point just ahead, not much higher than the surface.

3

I dream and the night fish come.
I tear my heart into pieces to feed them.

They like my heart and its slow currents,
the eroded banks where they might dig
a mud hole, a refuge, some darkness to defend.

ESSAY ON THE MODIFICATION OF CLOUDS

When you suddenly find your tongue twisted . . . as you seek
to explain to your six-year-old daughter why she can't go to
the public amusement park . . . and see tears welling up in
her eyes when she is told that Funtown is closed to colored
children, and see ominous clouds of inferiority beginning to
form in her little mental sky . . .
                                              —Martin Luther King, Jr.

1

Why? Maybe to foil restlessness or to make them settle.
And so their father taught them a magic trick:

how to make clouds disappear. "Watch. See that one?
I'll make it vanish." His gaze and then the empty air.

Cirrus. Cirrocumulus. Stratus. Cirrostratus. Stratocumulus.
Once there were no clouds, nothing that anyone called clouds, only essences.

In '64 or '65, a Black man believes he can make clouds disappear, altering
weather patterns in the Midwest and Johannesburg.

What are the origins of noctilucent clouds? Night clouds, night fingers,
blue-white fingers stroking a starlit wing.

Three Negro children in the back seat of a Chevy Bel Air beg their father
to make a cloud disappear. They never ask for the cloud's return.

2

In the movie, Moses stands beside the Israelites. A green-fingered
cloud comes out of the night. O children, who does death pass over?

Maybe our losses are insubstantial vapor. Adrift,
harried by winds, the past evaporates. The future condenses.

After her father's death, she studied the clouds, finding in their shape
lilies, a *running deer, a candle flame*, but nothing she would call *Daddy*.

Noctilucent—meaning night lace or night cloud, meaning moonlight
is sweetest when lapped from a Black woman's neck.

Meteorological studies reveal that memories are cloud formations,
disruptions of air patterns, coagulations of mist, wind currents.

3

What are clouds? Ice crystals, droplets of dew, condensations around
particulates of dust, or soot, or salt.

Mammatocumulus. Mammata. After a storm, mammata hang from a grey-green sky.
The earth suckles. The rain lies in pools of spilled milk.

Memory is the condensation of particulate matter, so small,
so small, so small, that it is felt only in its aggregations.

When he said ominous clouds of inferiority?
                    That was prophecy

He predicted storm? A deluge?

                    Storm is gonna come.
                    Say, a storm is gonna come.

4

What of clouds? Memory also dissipates, obscures, wanders, grows gravid
with humidity. In Nebraska, a child points to a cloud that bears her father's shape.

I wake to blindness. The light turns to gauze, to cottony billows. In my eyes there are swells of altocumulus and mist. Dry eye, the doctor says.

Clouds fade before a Black man's will. Belief in a man's will can make him God. Three Negro children know their father is God.

The clouds that you make vanish rise again, turn to lint inside your lungs, cloud-dust on your tongue. Your words are falling rain.

VI

Place here was all two-dimensional until it wasn't. All talk and icon and then the taste of a Macintosh apple.

—Kathleen Stewart

THE ART OF APPLE PEELING

1

A child stands in the kitchen of a one-bedroom flat
watching as her mother flays apples with a blade
no longer than an index finger, paring apples
while the pressure cooker's valve turns this way
round and that way back again to spit its hiss of steam.

On the counter, beside the stove, in a metal wash pan,
apples lie banked and glowing like embers, like lanterns
lifted by a mother's steady hands. Unfazed by brilliance
or heat, she trims their skins into scrolls, into scrim, thin,
thin, till the peels slip and spiral into her child's
cupped hands. Curled from her knife's lathe, there turns
a red road, a red flag, the apple's red tongue singing
of sweetness, of shape and boundary.

2

An apple turned and turning, centered in a woman's palm,
the cut and the wound, the knife pushed between pulp and peel,
the skin slowly shaved and slipped away—this is the art
of apple peeling. This is seduction and revelation that begins
with wounding. The peel winds round, spiraling, a moment
into other moments, sliding as a silk robe slides from a woman's
shoulder. The light that shines upon her bare skin is not the sun,
but the beloved who watches. The light that shines is her nakedness.
She is a colored woman. She shines. She shines apple bright.

3

In a kitchen, on the Black side of town, in a one-bedroom flat,
in '58 or '59, there is a child. She watches her mother.

The child is colored. The mother is yellow.
They have not yet removed their skins, nor will they.
But the child draws between her lips her mother's gift,
a ribbon, a well rope, a red string for a kite, an umbilical
cord, a helix coiling the way one thought coils around
another, a screwing spill like molasses from a biscuit sop
or spittle from slack lips. In the palm of a yellow woman
an apple lies plump as the *Grande Odalisque.* An apple sits
plump and smooth-skinned and shining upon a couch of flesh.

An apple's peeling is a curtain, a caul, a bounding wall.
What lies hidden beneath an apple's skin? Is desire
the gnawing worm or the worm bitten? Is it the worm-heart
curled in a womb of flesh or is it the apple heart that teaches
dimension: the death-worm that feeds unseen in what is,
at first, sweet, at first, for us alone, at first, safe? But it doesn't
matter. The mother will stab out the worm and worm-corrupted
parts and pitch the leavings into the pressure cooker, lesson learned.

4

Api Toile, Carpentin;
Foxwhelp, Sturmer;
Tremlett's Bitter, Gilpin;
Hauxapfel, Dulcet;
Early Joe, Anna;
Lady in the Snow, Toko;
Leather Coat, Mutsu;
Walter Please, Billie Bound;
Alexander, and Seek-No-Further.

5

Will you ever taste a *Shiawassee?*

6

If I say the sun hangs like a *Tallow Pippin*,

if I say its light is autumn cider or white vinegar,

if I say a heartbeat is the low note of windfall apples,

if I say there are more varieties of apples than of love, or if I say love resembles
       the slow art of apple peeling—requiring attention, a sharp edge, a
       wound, a revelation, and a falling away,

if I say the word of God is written not on a brittle scroll but on an apple
       peeling,

if the sum of all darkness is no bigger than an apple seed, and an apple's white
       meat is the sum of all light,

if I say the moon is only a peeled apple, the stars a glittery peel reeled into
       nebulae and constellation,

if I say I know this because I am Eve's daughter and have pressed an unpeeled
       apple against my thigh,

if I say I am the slayer of apples, have sucked apple peelings like the entrails of
       the sacrifice, have seen the death-worm and bitten it and swallowed but
       remember only the apple's sweetness,

if I say these words and hold in the palm of my hand an apple no bigger than
       a child's fist, an apple of mottled skin, smelling sweet, sweet, sweet, are
       you not tempted?

Notes

"Burn"

Where the fabric gapes . . . , from Roland Barthes, *The Pleasure of the Text*. 1973. Trans. Richard Miller. Hill and Wang, 1975: 9.

"Knowing How to Look"

Quotations from Langston Hughes, "Crossing." *The Collected Poems of Langston Hughes*. Ed. Arnold Rampersad and David Roessel. New York: Knopf, 1995: 251.

He was young . . . , from Oscar Micheaux, *The Homesteader*. Sioux City, IA: Western Book Supply, 1917: 22.

"When Identifying Tallgrass"

jump down turn around . . . , from a Black folksong.

"The Word You're Looking For"

What's the word . . . , from Carl Phillips, "What I See Is the Light Falling All Around Us," in *Wild Is the Wind*. Farrar Straus Giroux, 2018: 22.

"Yard Show I"

African American yard shows are powerfully rhetorical spaces . . . , from John Beardsley, "Salvage/Salvation: Recent African American Yard Shows." *American Sanctuary: Understanding Sacred Spaces*. Ed. Louis P. Nelson. Indiana University Press, 2006. 101.

What matters most is not to know the world but to change it . . . , from Frantz Fanon, *Black Skins, White Masks*. 1952. Trans. Charles Lam Markmann. Grove, 1967.

The interstate sliced . . . , from Paul Mullins, "Gardens in the Black City: Landscaping 20th-Century African America." paulmullins.wordpress.com/2015/07/19/gardens-in-the-black-city-landscaping-20th-century-african-america/

Perhaps everybody has a garden of Eden . . . , from James Baldwin, *Giovanni's Room*. 1956. Rpt. Delta, 2000: 25.

"Pausing Beside Her Yard"

Place is a pause in movement . . . , from Yi-Fu Tuan. *Space and Place: The Perspective of Experience*. Minneapolis: University of Minnesota Press, 1977: 138.

Is not the most . . . , from Roland Barthes, *The Pleasure of the Text*. 1973. Trans. Richard Miller. Hill and Wang, 1975: 9.

"The Art of Porch Swinging"

Scrubbed porches that sag . . . , from Lorraine Hansberry, *To Be Young, Gifted and Black: Lorraine Hansberry in Her Own Words*. 1969. Rpt. New York: Vintage, 1995: 17.

Talking softly . . . , from Gwendolyn Brooks, *Maud Martha*. 1953. Rpt. Chicago: Third World Press, 1993: 28.

"A Shining Lure"

Everything is about us . . . , paraphrasing from Daniel Spoerri, from *Trap-Pictures to Prillwitz Idols*. Cinisello Balsamo Milano: Silvana Editoriale, 2010: 115.

"On Seeing a Phasma Gigas"

Letter to Philip Rau, Oct. 29, 1914, from Charles H. Turner, Letters to Phil Rau. Edwin P. Meiners Collection. Folder 195. State Historical Society of Missouri.

"Yard Show II"

Without trouble, and death, no beauty . . . , from John Ruskin, *Modern Painters*. Vol 5. *The Works of John Ruskin*. Ed. E. T. Cook and Alexander Wedderburn. Longmans, Green, 1905: 98.

"There Is a Price"

Acka backa . . . , from a southern folk rhyme.

Bombingham. Nickname for Birmingham, Alabama during the Civil Rights Movement after a series of bombings from 1947 through 1965. Segregationists planted bombs to drive Black families out of white neighborhoods and in response to efforts to desegregate.

"What Place Is This, Where Are We Now?"

By prearranged signals . . . , from Owen W. Muelder, *The Underground Railroad in Western Illinois*. Jefferson, NC: McFarland, 2012: 75.

Phrases from "Grass," *The Complete Poems of Carl Sandburg*. New York: Houghton, Mifflin, Harcourt, 1970: 136.

A fusillade of pistols . . . , from Peter Friederici, *The Suburban Wild*. Athens: University of Georgia Press, 1999: 46.

"Memoir of a Heritage Tourist"

Colored People are bound . . . , from David W. Blight, *Frederick Douglass' Civil War: Keeping Faith in Jubilee*. LSU Press, 1991: 224.

"Pembroke Township, Illinois I"

an endless invisible present going on . . . , from C. S. Giscombe, *Giscome Road*. Dalkey Archive Press, 1998: 273.

Story: Sun and Moon asked . . . , Original retelling of "The Moon and Sun" in *African Tales: Folklore of the Central African Republic*. Ed. and trans. Polly Strong, ed. and illus. Rodney Wimer. Telcraft, 1992: 34.

Memory divides, then itself dogs all the shapes at once . . . , from C. S. Giscombe, *Here*. Dalkey Archive Press, 1994: 16.

Each landscape has a black edge to it . . . , from C. S. Giscombe, *Border Towns*. Dalkey Archive Press, 2016: 61.

"Through a Mobile Lens, Brooklyn, IL"

Home is not a place, but . . . an irrevocable condition . . . , from James Baldwin, *Giovanni's Room*. 1956. Rpt. Delta, 2000: 92.

I shall hold myself at liberty to speak . . . , Elijah Lovejoy quoted in Merton L. Dillon. *Elijah P. Lovejoy, Abolitionist Editor*. University of Illinois Press, 1961: 92.

"Flood Plains"

Italicized quotations from Eve Kosofsky Sedgwick, *The Weather in Proust*. Duke University Press, 2011: 84.

"Night Fishing"

In the cold spring night . . . , from "Smelt Fishing" in Robert Hayden, *Collected Poems of Robert Hayden*. Edited by Frederick Glaysher. New York: Liveright, 1985.

"If You Should Wake"

Everything in life dreams . . . , from Nilo Cruz, *Anna in the Tropics*. New York: Theatre Communications Group, 2003: 34.

"Essay on the Modification of Clouds"

When you suddenly find your tongue twisted . . . , from Martin L. King, "Letters From a Birmingham Jail" in *Why We Can't Wait*. Harper & Row, 1963: 83.

Acknowledgments

I am grateful to the editors who published the following poems, sometimes in earlier versions:

Academy of American Poets: Poem-a-Day: "Burn";
Beloit Poetry Journal: "Yard Show I";
Black Renaissance / Renaissance Noire: "Essay on the Modification of Clouds";
Callaloo: A Journal of African Diasporic Arts and Letters: "The Art of Apple Peeling";
Colorado Review: "On Seeing a Phasma Gigas";
Copper Nickel: "What Place Is This? Where Are We Now?";
Gulf Coast: "If You Should Wake";
The Gettysburg Review: "A Shining Lure";
The Journal: "Yard Show II";
Kenyon Review: "Through a Mobile Lens, Brooklyn, Illinois";
New Letters: "Prairie Blazing Star";
Poetry: "Wind Shear," "To the White Girl Who Told Me that Not Everything Is about Race," "Is It Beauty that We Owe?";
Prairie Schooner: "Memoir of a Heritage Tourist," "On the Road to the Old Negro Cemetery," "Night Fishing";
The Southern Review: "The Word You're Looking For";
Stand: "Anything Dark Bears the Name";
swamp pink: "Knowing How to Look," "Pembroke Township, Illinois."

To R.D.P. At the beginning and at the end.

To Anna I. Day, whose *wild imagination* has delighted so many.

To Molly MacRae and Elizabeth Hearne for reading and encouraging all the way.

Enduring gratitude to the John Simon Guggenheim Memorial Foundation, Cave Canem, the Creative Writing Program and the Department of English of the University of Illinois, and the many collectors of Black material culture who have saved and archived Black history across the Midwest.

A special thank you to the following readers for their insights, their questions, and their compasses: Martha Collins, Angie Estes, Ángel García, Michael

Hurley, Tyehimba Jess, Christopher Kempf, Dante Micheaux, Charles Rowell, Evie Shockley, Tom Sleigh, Elizabeth Spires, Corey Van Landingham, and with special gratitude to Peter Conners and BOA Editions.

I also want to thank the following people who offered feedback, provided resources, joined in my adventure, or allowed me to interview them about their lived experience: Angela J. Aguayo, George Almasi, Danotra Brown, Johari Cole-Kweli, Kristina Marie Darling, R. DeSande, Christopher Freeburg, Amy Hassinger, Trina Howard, Irvin J. Hunt, Allison Joseph, Brett Kaplan, Jeffrey Levine, Marva Nelson, Marcia Murphy, Ivory Pane, Goldie Robinson, Rashod Taylor, Veronica Thurman, Jordan Weber.

About the Author

With a heart divided between the Midwest and the South, Janice N. Harrington weaves memory and place into questions about how we build a sense of belonging. A Guggenheim fellow, winner of the Kate Tufts Discovery Award, and a Cave Canem fellow, Harrington has published three previous books of poetry: *Even the Hollow My Body Made Is Gone*, *The Hands of Strangers*, and *Primitive: The Art and Life of Horace H. Pippin*. Also an award-winning children's writer, Harrington teaches creative writing at the University of Illinois.

BOA Editions, Ltd. American Poets Continuum Series

No. 1 *The Fuhrer Bunker: A Cycle of Poems in Progress*
W. D. Snodgrass

No. 2 *She*
M. L. Rosenthal

No. 3 *Living With Distance*
Ralph J. Mills, Jr.

No. 4 *Not Just Any Death*
Michael Waters

No. 5 *That Was Then: New and Selected Poems*
Isabella Gardner

No. 6 *Things That Happen Where There Aren't Any People*
William Stafford

No. 7 *The Bridge of Change: Poems 1974–1980*
John Logan

No. 8 *Signatures*
Joseph Stroud

No. 9 *People Live Here: Selected Poems 1949–1983*
Louis Simpson

No. 10 *Yin*
Carolyn Kizer

No. 11 *Duhamel: Ideas of Order in Little Canada*
Bill Tremblay

No. 12 *Seeing It Was So*
Anthony Piccione

No. 13 *Hyam Plutzik: The Collected Poems*

No. 14 *Good Woman: Poems and a Memoir 1969–1980*
Lucille Clifton

No. 15 *Next: New Poems*
Lucille Clifton

No. 16 *Roxa: Voices of the Culver Family*
William B. Patrick

No. 17 *John Logan: The Collected Poems*

No. 18 *Isabella Gardner: The Collected Poems*

No. 19 *The Sunken Lightship*
Peter Makuck

No. 20 *The City in Which I Love You*
Li-Young Lee

No. 21 *Quilting: Poems 1987–1990*
Lucille Clifton

No. 22 *John Logan: The Collected Fiction*

No. 23 *Shenandoah and Other Verse Plays*
Delmore Schwartz

No. 24 *Nobody Lives on Arthur Godfrey Boulevard*
Gerald Costanzo

No. 25 *The Book of Names: New and Selected Poems*
Barton Sutter

No. 26 *Each in His Season*
W. D. Snodgrass

No. 27 *Wordworks: Poems Selected and New*
Richard Kostelanetz

No. 28 *What We Carry*
Dorianne Laux

No. 29 *Red Suitcase*
Naomi Shihab Nye

No. 30 *Song*
Brigit Pegeen Kelly

Colophon

BOA Editions, Ltd., a not-for-profit publisher of poetry
and other literary works, fosters readership and appreciation
of contemporary literature. By identifying, cultivating, and publishing both
new and established poets and selecting authors of unique literary talent,
BOA brings high-quality literature to the public.

Support for this effort comes from the sale of its publications, grant funding,
and private donations.

*

*The publication of this book is made possible, in part,
by the special support of the following individuals:*

Anonymous
Angela Bonazinga & Catherine Lewis
Mr. & Mrs. P. David Caccamise, *in memory of Dr. Gary H. Conners*
Daniel R. Cawley
Jonathan Everitt
Bonnie Garner
Margaret B. Heminway
Grant Holcomb, *in memory of Robert & Willy Hursh*
Kathleen C. Holcombe
Nora A. Jones
Christopher Kennedy
Paul LaFerriere & Dorrie Parini, *in honor of Bill Waddell*
Jack & Gail Langerak
Barbara Lovenheim
Joe McElveney
Boo Poulin
John H. Schultz
William Waddell & Linda Rubel
Michael Waters & Mihaela Moscaliuc